I Testify
Life is Forever

Growing Up in the Deep South
Poems and Short Stories

By

Curtis Malcolm Monroe Sr.

DORRANCE
PUBLISHING CO
EST. 1920
PITTSBURGH, PENNSYLVANIA 15238

Dorrance Publishing Co
585 Alpha Drive
Pittsburgh, PA 15238
Visit our website at *www.dorrancebookstore.com*

ISBN: 979-8-89027-272-0
eISBN: 979-8-89027-770-1

The Cooks of Thompson, AL

As I sit here and I look back, why did my mother have to come home so late very night? While my mother was off cooking somebody else's food, we were at home, doing the best we could. Now remember we were just two little boys. We had an old wood stove. We had to cut the wood, clean the ashes out, and make a fire. Sometimes, when it would rain, a leaking roof would put the fire right back out.

Growing up, we ate a lot of cold food. So we had to eat whatever we could find. So we had to go out and raid people's farms. Mr. Marshall had a watermelon patch. Mr. Tee had the cantaloupe. Mr. Bob Todd had the corn. Mr. Putt had the sugarcane. Mr. Fate Jackson had the peaches that would melt in your mouth. We had plums and blackberries too. Miss Addie had a big pear tree. Down in Miss Fannie's pasture, there was a lot of mush dime.

We ate a lot of wild game. Squirrel, rabbit, opossum, beaver, and muskrat. Sometimes the Pete Time Boys would roll by selling black birds. Yes, we ate them too. But the cooks that worked with my mother always came through.

Miss Bennie would always bring us chicken and dumplings just about every day, also what they did not eat every day. Miss Bennie's housekeeping was a part of her job, as well as taking care of other people's kids. She worked all her life. She would never forget to bring us some food. Miss Jessie looked out for my mother too. She would go in the smokehouse just about every other day and give my mother some meat, just to make sure we had something to eat. She did this for us. I do not know anyone else with such a beautiful soul, and she was always with a smile. Miss Jessie, I will never forget you.

Miss Catherine was the cook who worked in the same house as my mother did. She also made sure we had something to eat. She was a heavy lady, and she was mean, but Miss Catherine could cook some beautiful corn-bread and black-eyed peas. She ran a shot house on the side. Mr. Euggie

Brown had one eye because she had stabbed him in the eye. No matter what she did, she made sure we were fed.

To all the cooks and mothers who look out for us, I will love you forever. "That will do, Curt. That will do."

Written by
Curtis Monroe,
Alabama

Where Have All the Americans Gone?

I welcome you to Mexico Springs; the city of Union Springs is under siege. The City Council is at each other's throats. The mayor spent his time trying to grab a woman's butt. Gang members are shooting up the streets, young girls are selling their bodies while law enforcement sleeps. Meanwhile, people we have never seen before are now controlling the streets. Selling pinatas on South Main Street while their children run wild at the grocery stores. To all the Black people who live in Mexico Springs, our name has been changed. Buddy is our name now. Disrespected just to buy gas and beer. Most of us don't say a thing. We don't worship the Monkey God Rat and creepy things. We worship a Living God. It's a shame to see you do the things you do lining up to kiss their asses.

We as Black people have been pushed enough that we refused to be pushed any more. Make fun of me and call me stupid and dumb. American! That's who I am! When it's all said and done, how many Americans will be left? If you want someone to blame, look in the mirror and you will see yourself. See no evil, see nothing. Hear no evil, hear nothing. Speak no evil, speak nothing. Tomorrow morning, we will see the sunrise. The wind will blow like it always has; thousands of people will still pass away. It will not matter if I like you or not. It will not matter what I think of you, but what you think of me. Arrogant and racist. That is who you are. Who taught you to hate people you don't even know? Maybe that briefing you got down at the rattlesnake church doesn't work anymore. Maybe you should go back and get bit some more. I got some advice for you. You come to my country, but you don't pay any taxes, but I do. I wish I was in Dixie. Hooray! Hooray! Look away, Dixieland. What used to be Dixie, ain't no more! Where have all the Americans gone? I hear the Rio Grande has dried up. It has been rerouted behind a local hardware store. Maybe all the Americans should pack up and move to the Mexico. Soon, in Alabama there will not be any more room for you or for me to live. Only for people who have a red dot in the middle of their head. I wish, I wish, I was in Dixie. Look away. Look away. Dixie is gone and won't be back. Who is gonna fight in the next Civil War? Look away, look away. Dixie is gone.

Maybe when the City Council gets their ducks in a row, they will get a red dot in the middle of their heads. They will vote to change the name to Mexico Springs. But before all the Americans get out of Union Springs, someone will have to grab the American Flag. Look away, look away. Dixie is gone. Now, learn Dixie in Spanish and Arabic.

I Love Alabama, but not the Hate!

When I think of Alabama, why do you think our state is Number One? We run and jump better than anyone. Remember Jesse Owens in the Olympic Games? When he showed the world that people from Alabama were number one. Showed Adolf Hitler where he was from. What about Joe Louis, our Native Son from Alabama, King of the Ring. The Bear with a checkerboard hat took the sideline. We all know he was the chosen one. I love Alabama with all my heart. I love the state but not the hate. Think of all the wonderful people we got, and we all love a good fight. We got in our heart, but some of it has been misplaced down through history. We did a lot of things wrong. We helped turn human beings into slaves and beat them with whips and put them in chains. But all of that was a long time ago. But in this time and day all that hate has not gone away. I love Alabama but not the hate.

John Lewis went to walk across a bridge, and Alabama State Troopers tried to take his life away. His blood still remains a stain on that bridge to this very day. All this blood just to vote and let little children go to a good school. Somebody placed a bomb and just blew them away. Some of them just wanted to sit down and eat a good meal. The police showed up and beat them up with sticks. Roll Tide, why did you want to go? Just wanted to have a better life. It took the National Guard to move hate out of the way!

Roll Tide, roll them out the way! Roll Tide, roll away all their hopes and dreams out of the way. Roll Tide, and answer me this, why is a grandmother going after our votes again? Roll Tide, roll all the hate away, but every Sunday you yell your head off while the big elephant rolls everybody teams out the way. I love Alabama, like most of us do. Why can't we enjoy it just like you do? I like to fish all the time. It helps me to relax and clear my mind. I love to hunt and spend time in the woods watching the little squirrels and deer running around. They also make a good meal. This is what our great state is all about. It's all about love and not the hate.

Now don't you think we have been divided for too long? Take a long look and tell me what you see? Another generation is on the way. Don't you want to get along? They are not Black, they are in the middle, they are just right.

Why is this guy walking around with a gun on his side? He sure doesn't look like a cop. Tattoos running down both of his arms. I look everywhere; I don't see a badge on him anywhere; now don't get mad with me. I only write about what I see. People of color could get shot down anywhere. Me, myself, looked for somewhere I could run. I was looking for an exit door. Mass killing is now a common thing. Somebody looking to take other people's lives away. Alabama, so I have heard, has an open-carry law on the books. Meet me in the streets at high noon. We are going to do this the Cowboy way! No place for love. No place for grace. No place for forgiveness. No place for the next generation. Will they learn to love, or will they be taught to hate? A local TV station will cover the news. They will tell the story of how hate will run your life. We all breathe the same air. I love Alabama with all my heart. I love the state but not the hate.

Big Man Woman

Big man woman in the corner in the back, in the dark. We were all at the Honky Tonk that Saturday night, just shooting pool and getting drunk. Slowly the door opened up. It was Big Man and his woman, Boo. They both dressed as sharp as a tack. Boo sure was looking good, long black pretty hair. Tight blue jeans that fit everywhere, had on the prettiest little white shoes, a pretty red bow on the side. Big man sat her on her throne. He wiped the seat off first and then sat her down. She had a brown bag in her hand where she carried Big Man's gun. I thought about the song the old ladies sing in church every Sunday morning. It had gotten late in the evening, and the sun was going down. The music got loud, and everyone hit the dance floor. It was time to get down! B.B. King was on the box, and for two people this would soon be true. Bro Tuttle and Ned hit the door where they stood, so drunk they could not drink any more. They had been out in the woods all night long.

They looked like two boogiemen, with their hair not combed, ratty old dirty clothes, shoes so old you could see their feet, and they smelled so bad that the birds started to fall from the trees. B.B. King was getting down, and Big Man got up and went to the bathroom. Bro Tuttle and Ned got up and started to do their thing. They both started to play their invisible instruments. One played the drums, while the other played the guitar. They were playing so hard, they forgot where they were at. They had gotten too close to Big Man's woman's chair. Boo just sat there and did not move. She had to be thinking, *What's wrong with these two fools?*

They had just broken the golden rule. They were trying to pull Boo out of her chair. One on the right and one on the left, trying to make her get up and dance. We ran over and tried to pull them back. We felt they were safe, so we let them go. By this time Big Man stepped out the bathroom door, looked over, and saw what was going on. We saw death on his face. Bro Tuttle and Ned were standing at the devil's door. He had one of them in one hand and pinned the other one to the wall with the other hand. They both started to scream and shout. Then they realized there was no way out. He slammed both of them so hard to the floor that I saw a little pee fall to the floor. He threw them around like two rag dolls. We ran over and pulled Big Man off, trying to give Ned and Bro Tuttle a way out.

There was no way out of the door. All the windows were nailed closed. The only way out was through the floor, so they started pulling nails out with their teeth. After they got the nails out, they started pulling out the wood with their hands and feet. So, we turned Big Man loose one more time. There was only the dirt left, and they turned into two black moles before our faces. One dug on the right and the other dug on the left. There was so much dirt in the air you couldn't see where they were at. They dug their way out, but it was not over yet. Both of their belts had gotten caught on a nail. Big Man walked up with a two-by-four; it was time for ass and elbow. Big Man walked up behind Bro Tuttle first and hit him so hard, a burst of gas filled the air. Then it was Ned's turn; a loud burst of gas knocked us all back. Just for fun, somebody lit a match and a burst of flames shot out. They left out of there like two shooting stars and were never heard from or seen again.

John the Baptist

There was a man named John; they say he was a prophet's son. He had a cousin who would be as famous as he. Now John would tell a great story, too. He would tell the world about who would come. He preached to everyone who would hear him. The Lamb of God would be the one. He ran around half-naked all the time. He lived in the wilderness and had a few good men who followed him around. He hung around where the water was. John's job was to baptize and let everybody know soon the Romans would not have much to say. He ate wild honey and locusts too. Every day he stood in the hot sun and called to let him put some water on you. "What I will give you will set you free. There's a guy named Herod who doesn't like me. He is going to do everything he can to get rid of me."

Then one day as he stood and preached to the crowd, he saw a man walking in the light. He walked to the edge of the waterline and said to John, "Baptize me, the Lamb of God," looking right into his face. John took him down under the waves, and when he brought him up, a couple of doves filled the space. Then the Lamb of God made his way, going to do what his father told him to do. Now John the Baptist had said some really mean things about Herod the King. So some of the things were all true. He talked about how Herod had taken his brother's wife and made her his. He said the King was no good and had a child out of wedlock. Now old Herod had heard what John had said; his wife wanted John's head. So, Herod told John he had better shut up. "I will send my soldiers out and lock you up." John did not care what Herod said; he was going to preach until he was dead. John had said too much. Herod sent his men out and brought John in and put him in the castle jail. One night when his wife went to sleep, Herod went down to give John a speech. While he was down in John's cell, someone was eavesdropping and heard what he had said. Now Herod was afraid of John and didn't want him to be killed and let him go free. His wife and daughter still wanted John dead. Everyone had heard what John had said,

"Repent! Repent! The coming of the Lord is at hand." While John was locked up behind the castle walls, the Lamb of God came to see him. John asked the Lamb of God just one thing, "Are you the one or will another one come after you?" He then let John know that he was the one. And with that, both had to travel down the path given to them by God. King Herod threw a big party the following night, and everyone came. All the kings and queens came from everywhere. They got drunk and started to dance. Herod got drunk and wanted his stepdaughter to dance for him.

He told her he would give her anything, even up to half of his kingdom. Her mother was there too, and she called her daughter to the back, and they hatched a plan. When she came back, Herod asked the same question again, "Name it! Whatever you ask of me I will do!"

She looked him straight in his eyes and said, "John the Baptist's head." Herod was shocked at what she had said. What could she do with a dead man's head? His word was given to her, and there was no way out of what he had said. What would the other kings and queens say? He told his guard to bring out John. This would be the day he would die.

Down to the dungeon they went. They cut John's head off and gave it to her. They say Herod went mad after that. John had completed his mission, and then he left. The Lamb of God will carry his cross all by himself.

Jesus, Son of a Living God

Twinkle, twinkle, little star, three wise men came from so far, all of them following a bright star. On their way to find the king; a small child was sent from beyond the Milky Way.

A young maiden in a faraway land was about to give the whole world the son of man.

Born in a smelly place, wild animals standing around eating hay, and then the three wise men came and knelt before the king. When King Herod heard about all of this, he wanted to know where he was at. He sent his soldiers out to take his life away, but his father who sat about the clouds sent an angel down and told his earthly father to get out of town. When the king passed away, the angel went and told his parents it was safe to go back home. He spent his time being a carpenter's son.

When the time was right, they went on their way. He knew about his cousin John. It was time to hunt him down. He knew it was time to get baptized. Time to be dipped in the water and clean his soul. He walked out in the desert to take Satan, and after he beat Satan at his own game, he proved to him he could not be deceived at all. Then he went down to the river shore and found twelve men who would follow him. He showed up to a party where his mother was at, and they ran out of wine. His mother told him to touch the water and turn it to wine and make it so good they would never forget his first miracle. There were a lot of people there who witnessed the power of a living God. He took his twelve, and they walked away. They walked the dusty roads at night and day. He performed miracle after miracle everywhere they went.

He gave the ability to see again.

He set a parasite free and brought a small child back to life.

He gave a mother her son back.

He drove out the evil of a living soul.

He called fish from the bottom of the sea.

He taught twelve men how to live like him.

He made the crippled walk again and fed the multitude of people from two loaves of bread and fish to make it a meal.

He spoke to the sea and made the waves calm down.

He told the wind not to blow anymore; "Peace be still," was all he said.

The thunder and lightning went away.

He took the time to teach men and women how to pray.

He walked on water, and his feet never got wet.

He gave mankind the power to run the devil away.

He performed many miracles that were not written down.

Oh yeah, I forgot; he raised his friend Lazarus from the grave as well.

When he walked into his father's house, he ran the money changer out. Showed their buddies the front door. When he got there the Romans knew everything that Jesus had done. The High Priest wanted Jesus dead. He said he was turning people against Rome. They put their heads together and came up with a plan to make Jesus look bad. They had a big court and wanted to condemn him in front of people. They came in and told a lot of lies, but a lot of people were already on Jesus's side. They took him to Pilard, the man in charge, but he did not want to take his life. They took him to the Jews' King but were afraid of him, so he sent him back. The Priest said he must die. The Roman in charge sent him out to be beat, but that was not good enough for the High Priest. The Roman in charge said he would let the people make the choice. They took him out before the crowd along with a really bad boy and told the crowd to decide which one of them should live or die. Some of them cried out in Jesus's name, but the other part of the crowd yelled for the bad guy. The Roman said, "Jesus must die." The Roman soldiers made him a big wooden cross and put a crown of thorns on top of his head, and they beat him before they walked him out. He carried it all the way to the top of the hill. They threw him on the cross and tied both of his hands and then his feet to it. They then took out three steel spikes, and with his hand outstretched and one powerful blow, the spikes went through his right hand. He cried out in terrible pain. They then moved to the left hand, and it received the same treatment. All this pain for the sin of man; with one spike left, they moved down to his feet, which they stacked one on top of the other, and they drove the spike right into both feet. That pain was heard around the world. So much pain for ungrateful men. His mother stood at the bottom of his cross and watched her son take his last breath and die. "I will rise in three days and the twelve will watch me go back to where I came from."

Curtis Malcolm Monroe Sr.

If it Had Not Been for Jesus

If it had not been for Jesus, where would I be?

Somewhere out walking the streets alone, looking for crack all night long.

Broke and all my paycheck gone, all of my family at home,

Waiting for me to come back home.

Did not have any food to eat, no money for gas, and couldn't even buy children school clothes.

I could not stop smoking crack until all of my money was gone.

Wearing dirty clothing and ratty shoes. Being laughed at by people driving their cars.

I could hear what they were thinking as they passed by me: *I am not going to put a crackhead in my car*. One Saturday night, I was walking home, full of crack and alcohol too. I could not have walked another step, and I looked over my shoulder; there was a house of God standing there. I walked over there and knocked on the door, and they let me stay there. I slept there all night, but there were other nights where I had to sleep in a city dump. I lay right down on the ground; snakes and bugs were crawling all around.

God sent his angels, and they encircled me and kept me safe. There was the time when my car broke down, and I was out there, high on crack, walking, again asking myself if I needed to find a place to sleep. So he showed me an old house sitting on a hill. I walked into the house and could not see a single thing. Through a small crack in the wall, I saw a beam of light. The floor was dirty and full of trash everywhere. There was an old sofa turned upside down in the middle of all this mess. I flipped it over and slept there all night. There had to be all kinds of snakes in that house. He sent his angels, and they protected me as I lay there.

All power, all glory belongs to him and him alone. He took care of me, and he has never left me alone. Then my wife put me out. Here I am again without a home. Then all of my sin caught up with me, and it was time for me to go to jail and pay for all of my sins. They catch up with me every now and then, lying, stealing, and cheating too. I had to jump out of some windows when their husbands came home late.

I must have gone to jail at least twenty-five or thirty times. A little voice came to me one night while I was in jail and told me to stop my evil ways or I would go to Hell. So I picked up the Bible and started to read it while on my lunch break. I read it on my break, and when I got off of work, I read it all night long. As I was lying down to sleep one night, an angel of God came and stood over my bed, and to my surprise, I woke up praising his holy name. When I told some of my so-called friends, they did not believe a single thing I told them. All my bad habits went away.

I did not need crack any more.

The nicotine urge went away, and I threw away all of my cigarettes that were in my house.

I did not want gin any longer, or moonshine. I kicked it all out!

The pot I smoked for so long was no longer a welcomed guest in my home.

I hired the Budweiser horses to come and take away all of my beer.

His word really did heal me now.

I am really free.

I don't lie any more.

I don't cheat any more.

I don't steal any more.

I don't hate any more.

Now I can really say how much I love a living God.

I love him in the morning.

I love him in the noon day.

I love him when I speak.

I love him when I sleep.

I love him more than my children.

I love him more than my wife.

I love him more than life.

Curtis Malcolm Monroe Sr.

The Jungle Lover

I just saw a Black man flying through the trees. Doing a flip from tree to tree. He did not make a single noise. This guy had hardly any clothes on at all. A flap in the front and a flap in the back. He looked to be about six foot three and had big muscles everywhere. Then one of the chiefs popped up and said, "I heard about this man, how he would swing down from the trees and pick my daughter up. She had her grass skirt in her hand. She said he was one hell of a man. He took her to his tree, and they made wild love all night long. He would grab a vine and bring her back home."

The air was hitting me in my face. My hair was all over the place. He whispered in my ear and told me his name. "I am the Tree Top Lover; a.k.a. Jungle Lover is my nickname. I travel all over the place. A lot of jungle girls know my name. I am your jungle love for one night. I travel with the moonlight, standing out by your hut. Just call out my name, 'Jungle Lover, where are you? I want to go to your tree house tonight and do my thing! Wing down, baby, and pick me up!'" Then his name had got around to all the little jungle towns. Then all the drums started to talk, for all the people to know the jungle lover took my daughter away. Late last night, flying through the trees, late at night that boy got some red-hot jungle love. Lock your daughter up and put a guard outside of your hut! If we catch you, Jungle Lover, we are going to beat you up, then we are going to burn you up. Then we are going to burn your treehouse down. We don't care if you are the king, son!

Yes, we know about your little chimp friends you have been hanging out with down at the lion's den. Some more of your savage friends. And all the elephants have been lining up, bragging about how they have your back. Those little girls you swooped down on, running through the jungle, looking for you late at night.

What did you do to those little girls' daddies? Have put warpaint on out at night looking for you. Say they are going to make a little girl and your mother sit in the hut and cry all night, "Jungle Lover, Jungle Lover, Jungle Lover, fly by my hut tonight, swing down and pick me up and give me a ride on that vine. Set me free, Jungle Lover. Come and play with me."

Laquitta, the Queen of the H Mama

I am six foot two and weigh one hundred and thirty pounds.

There's not a man born who can match up with me.

Never seen a man I could not beat.

And that's from the bedroom to the street.

Who am I? What am I?

Listen to me and I will make it clear. I Laquitta, the Hoogie Mama Queen.

Bad to the bone. When I walk the streets, the dogs and cats bow.

All the squirrels run up their trees and hide.

I don't have a mouth full of gold teeth.

I don't need a body full of silicone. All of my behind is all mine.

I don't get drunk in other women's faces.

The sun doesn't come up until I come outside.

My sister's name is Pluto.

My brother's name is Mars.

I have held the Milky Way in my hands.

I used a living star as an earring.

They threw me out of Heaven before I got my wings.

I went down to Hell where I lived for a day.

The Devil came and told me, "Honey, you got to go.

All of my demons don't want you here anymore."

I sailed in the trees of Africa while riding on a vine with Black Tarzan holding me on his side.

When I got ready to leave, he cried like a child and fell down on his knees and kissed my behind.

Who am I? What am I?

What am I?

My name is Laquitta.

I am the Hoogie Mama Queen.

Don't ever disrespect me! I will take your soul.

I can hear men screaming out my name from a hundred miles away.

All of the women from around the way make fun of my name, but you can't pay them a million dollars to do it to my face.

When I come to town all the men leave their wives.

They stumble around my yard all day and night.

Honey, I have to call the police to break up all the fights.

They peep through my windows just to catch a glimpse and try to see just what I got.

Sometimes they get so hot that they burst into flames.

The fire department has a truck parked at my back door.

I went to church a very long time ago.

The angels came down from Heaven just to sing for me.

They gave me milk and honey to help me go to sleep.

Who am I? What am I?

I am Laquitta, the Hoogie Mama Queen.

I can remember a long time ago when I used to ride the pole.

When I walked up on stage, laid my hands around that pole, lightning would come down and strike it.

It would turn into a flame of fire while the Devil worked the door.

When I started moving, I could make my booty sing.

The lights went out, and all the nails came out of the floor.

All the windows shattered, and glass went everywhere.

All of the bottles behind the bar got up and sang.

All of the girls in the back started to shout out my name!

They all took their things off and nailed them to the door.

They all came out with their hands held high and pleaded to the queen, "We will never dance here anymore."

Who am I? What am I?

Then I asked them what my name was.

Who am I?

What am I?

I am Laquitta, the Hoogie Mama Queen!

Curtis Malcolm Monroe Sr.

Mixed and Divided

Put together, combine, blend, mingle.

They are not white. They are not white.

They are in the middle. They are in the middle. They are just right.

In the beginning all women and men were of one skin and were of one tongue.

God sent down his word that broke them up, and from that day on they wander to all different parts of the Earth.

Some went to the North. Some went to the South. Some went to the East, and some went to the West.

That's where all this stuff of skin color came about. You are black. You are brown. You are white. You are yellow, and the rest of you can just get in line.

Your eyes are round. Your eyes are slanted. I don't want my daughter to marry your kind.

You got big lips and nappy short hair. As you can see, my hair is straight and falls to the side.

I got red hair, blond hair too. A small nose and tiny lips to parts of the body will not work for you.

My heart, my eyes, my brain, my liver, my kidney, and other body parts will only work with somebody who is white. Your body parts will only work with somebody who is black.

My God is white with pretty blond hair.

Your God is black with high, tight hair.

My God can walk on water.

My God can part the red sea.

My God's word can raise a man from the dead.

Now tell me what your God can do.

Your God let you be a slave for all them years.

My God put me in charge, and I told you what to do.

My God gave me a better brain.

Your God would not let you read or write.

Now that we have gotten all of that out of the way, color should not matter, anyway.

Listen to all the different ways we talk.

Maybe we should find a way to communicate better.

Your tongue is white, and my tongue is black.

The air you breathe is white, and the air I breathe is black.

We are not white.

We are not black.

We were all made by God.

We are all just right?

The Big Shot Church

I went up north and worked all my life. Now I am taking my wife and kids and moving back down South.

Going to show all them poor Black folks what a living I got.

I hear some of them still got an outhouse.

I retired from my job yesterday. Got a pocket full of money and a brand-new car. Going back home in the Deep South.

I got a beautiful wife at my side. Three beautiful children going down for the ride. All of my children have a college degree.

They are not as black as me. They took after their mother's side. She is as light yellow as she can be.

Going to build me a big brick home out in the countryside.

Gonna have a lot of security to keep the locals out. Don't come out to see what I do.

Gonna find me a nice big church to go to. I was told a lot of people just like me, people who just retired and moved back from up north who got a lot of money to give to God. I'm gonna wear a five-hundred-dollar suit, gator shoes, a pure silk, mostly blue tie.

Gonna find us a preacher who knows the word of God. A man who can put the devil under his feet.

Gonna put five hundred dollars on his collection plate. A man who put the riff raff out.

I don't want no broke man looking at my fine light-skin wife.

As we all gathered for church one beautiful Sunday morning, we all heard this man singing this made-up song.

"My name is Johnny Mack. I got drunk, and I was walking all night." As we looked up to see who he was, we could all see a pitiful sight. Old dirty hat, holes had taken the clothes he wore. He looked as though he hadn't combed his hair in a year. As he got closer to where we were, we could smell the moonshine and gin on his breath. He smelled so bad some of the birds fell out of the air.

"My name is Johnny Mack. I got drunk, and I have been walking all night."

I heard one of the deacons say, "You cannot come to our church, anyway.

If one of you be with sin, take your Bible and toss my word out of your hand."

And then they all ran into the church. One of the ushers locked the gate.

After all of them got back in, they all began to preach and shout, thanking God for all they had.

Somewhere they lost their hearts.

God had given all the good things of his world, but they were not willing to let the poor Johnny Mack have a seat in the house of God.

As they got in their brand-new cars and went back to their fine brick homes, I am willing to bet you they will never forget the Johnny Mack song.

My name is Johnny Mack. I got drunk, and now I have to walk all night.

Curtis Malcolm Monroe Sr.

My Big Brother and the Swimming Hole

I have a story to tell you about when I was growing up. Right after we left Sunday school, we would run home and change out clothes and rush down to the swimming hole. My little brother and some of our friends would run down the hill while taking off their clothes and go swimming in the nude. Now this hole was full of snakes. These snakes were of the deadly kind and ruled the pond. They did not like us hanging around, and if they bit you, you would surely die.

We were a bunch of wild little country boys who did not give a damn. Back in the day, on Sunday afternoon, all of the young men would be out walking their girlfriends around. Now we have been warned more than a hundred times, "Don't be out there swimming in the nude when we come by walking our girlfriends around."

"You are not our daddy; you don't tell us what to do." It had got a little, so it was time for a lunch break. So, we decided to go down and eat some plums. When we got our bellies full, we thought we would stop by Mr. Manshell's watermelon patch. Well, Mr. Manshell had warned from time to time what he would do to us if he ever caught us in his watermelon patch. Again, he went and told our mother he was going to poison us if he saw us in his field stealing again.

We were a bunch of wild little country boy;, we did not give a damn what Mr. Manshell had said, and if he messed with us, we would tell the police where he got his whiskey still hidden.

So when we decided to leave, we went to Miss Fannie Todd's land and sat up in the trees while we ate some muscadine. We played as Tarzan and swung from the vine, and from there we went to visit the Pete Time Boys. The Pete Time Boys lived deep in the woods. They lived so far back that sometimes they could not even get sunlight. There were fifteen boys and one girl. The Pete Time Boys were known for picking cotton: 165 bales in one year. Fifteen Tasmanian devils in the field with a cotton sack on their back. It was like a bomb had been dropped in the field. All you saw was dust. It was brutal. Two of their mules had a heart attack from trying to keep up with them. So when we got to the top of the hill, it looked like somebody was standing on the top of the house. They had both of his arms stretched out, so, when we made it to the house, we asked why was Load standing on top of the house? To our surprise the Pete Time Boys got electric lights and a black-and-white television set. But it didn't come with an antenna, so they couldn't see what was on the TV.

So somebody had to stand on top of the house and hold both of the antenna wires, so the family could see the TV. Sometimes a storm would come up, and sometimes someone got struck by lightning, explaining why they looked the way they did. We looked around a little more. Where in the bell did the Pete Time Boys get a car from? The first time they had seen one, it was on TV. That car looked just like Fred Flintstone's car. So they gathered up the material and they made themselves one. It had stone tires just like his. An old bedsheet hanging off the top, didn't have a floor at all, two wooden boards made up the seats, and a handlebar was the steering wheel; their feet were used as the motor. They had a water bucket on the frame so that when they stopped, they used the water to cool their feet off. It was time to go, and we had seen enough. We laughed so hard we couldn't speak.

It was time to get one last swim in at the swimming hole. When we got back to the swimming hole and took off our clothes and jumped in, we saw my big brother and all of his friends lining up, and we saw our daddy come down and get all of our clothes. All of them had a big scrap in their hands, and we knew they had come to beat the hell out of us. There was only one way out, and that was a big blackberry bush. We could hear our mothers calling out our names. Now it was time to do or die, and we didn't have anything on! It was time to run the gauntlet! So I took off as fast as I could. Five of the boys on both sides; my brother hit me so hard he almost knocked the wind out of me. When I got up, I had stickers in my mouth, my hair, my tongue, my feet, and my nose. I don't know where my clothes were. When I got home my mother had them in her hand. I could not lay down. I could not sleep, and to the very day some of the blackberry bushes still remind me, *don't go swimming on Sunday!*

Curtis Malcolm Monroe Sr.

This Jimmy Loves Anchorman

Here at NNC News

The Statue of Liberty

We here at NNC have just received a special news report. The Statue of Liberty wants to talk! I'd be damned if I didn't know she could talk. We jumped in the news truck and took off. But a whole lot of other news people had beat us there. As we pulled up it was an amazing sight to see. She lifted her dress a little bit, and then she started to walk down the steps. Her foot touched the water first, then the right foot followed. She stood in the middle of the harbor and just looked at us. She waded out in the water about waist deep. Then we could see the tears rolling down her face. We saw a little faint smile and a cute twinkle in her eye. She looked around a bit and took off her crown and laid it to the side. That big book she held so close to her chest, she released into the water, and it just floated away. The torch that she held so tight in her big hand, she lifted it up very high, and out came a flame with a big blow of air, and the flame went out. She then walked out of the harbor and put both of her feet on solid ground. All the newspeople took a step back, as her lips started to move a little bit. She only said two words. She looked us straight in the face and said, "I QUIT!" She then said a few more words, "No questions from the press today. I just want you to listen to what I have to say. Would one of you guys put a microphone on me and come in closer to me? I want the whole world to hear and see me. I am a woman, as you all can see. I am out here in the harbor all night and all day. Look at what this weather has done to me! I would like to get a perm every now and then; maybe then I could get a man! You know, right now as I stand here and speak, homeless people are living in my torch. The smog I have to smell is burning my eyes so bad I can't see. And when the virus struck, they came out and put a giant mask on me. Right now, I can't even scratch my nose! I can't sleep at night with all those damn boats blowing their little horns every day and night. I am so stiff I cannot move at all. I can't even get a pair of brand-new shoes. A pair of earrings sure would look great. I got to pee so bad, and I haven't taken a dump in fifty years. I quit! I am tired of all this shit! Send me back home all the way to France. I got a taste for some snails and a tall glass of champagne. America, why do you hate so much? Hate so thick I can smell it all the way up here. I never thought at all that I would see people with guns shooting at me. What in the hell is going on, people shooting each other down in the street. It got so bad it is not safe for kids to go to school! What has happened to the country I grew to love so much. Where human life doesn't mean a thing.

"I QUIT! I QUIT! I QUIT! I QUIT!

"I love the people of this country who welcome everybody in giving them the freedom to live and grow.

"But if I could live as a human for one day, there are a few things I would like to say. Listen.

To hear a small bird sing a beautiful song.

"To hear the laughter of a small child as they play.

"To touch the skin of another human being.

"To fly on an airplane and travel to lands far away.

"To hold a crying baby in my arms.

"To wake up from a long night's sleep and have the sunlight in my face.

"To make love to a man all night long.

"To live in a real house and call it home.

"To have a child and call it my own.

"To eat a Big Mac and wipe ketchup from my face.

"To go to a beauty salon and stay there all day long.

"To ride a horse out into a grassy field.

"To go to a zoo and look a lion right in the face.

"To sit on a toilet stool and take a long pee.

"To have someone to sit me down and tell me all about this spirit they call God.

"To see the White House in all its glory and understand its story.

"America, I love you with all my heart that beats in me.

"I will go back now and take my place, and when all the ships come sailing by, they all know I am the Statue of Liberty!"

Don't go, just don't go out

Don't go to the movies, you might get shot.
Don't go to church, someone will walk out of the darkness with a different plot.
Don't go to a baseball game, no one will be there to play.
A different kind of virus has run all the players far away.
Don't go to visit Grandmama at the nursing home, you will only see them pass away through a thick piece of glass.
Don't let your children go to school, there will be parents outside screaming and cutting a fool about all of the rules.
Don't go to the grocery store, the prices are too high, and hate will walk the aisle with color on its mind.
If your skin color is black, you better run and hide.
Don't go, just don't go.
Don't go to take a flight on an airplane, you better wear a mask, or they'll throw you off that plane fifty thousand feet in the sky.
Everybody fussing and fighting all the way down the aisle, you better hope Mike Tyson is not on your flight.
Don't go to the beach, the great whites live out there.
They're hungry too, because all of the pollution has killed their food.
All of them pretty asses go swimming by, what's a shark to do?
All young and tender, look good to the great white.
What's a shark to do?
Don't go, just don't go outside in the sun. It is really beaming down.
Don't go to the North Pole, all of the ice has melted away.
Poor polar bears don't have nowhere to stay.
Niagara Falls has dried up too.
All the fish have packed up and left too.
Don't go out looking for some gas, they are all sold out.
Tell me, people, do you remember how to ride a mule?

Don't go out, just don't go out looking for your family or your friends,
they all are standing in line, looking to the sky, saying Amen.
Don't go out, just don't go out, but I know you got to.

Eve, the first bBack woman and Adam called his wife
Named Eve because she was the Mother of all Living.
A Black woman walked in the Garden of Eden and talked to God.
She was there from the start.
Her skin was black, maybe even brown. Her eyes were like the brightness of the moon.
Made by the hands of a living God, took a rib and gave it a heart.
Gave Adam his first son, Mother of all living men to walk to earth.
The first woman to till the soil.
The first woman to make clothing to wear. She was the first woman to comb her hair.
The first woman to have sex with a man.
The first woman to pull an apple off of a tree.
The first woman to cry.
The first woman who had a child to die.
She helped Adam give all the animals names.
The first woman to see the sunrise. She watched as God put the Stars in the sky.
She saw the Angels when they came flying by.
Adam lived for 930 years and fathered fifty-six children.
The Bible doesn't say how long Eve would live, but it doesn't matter anyway. She was the Mother of all living men.
She was a Black woman.

Curtis Malcolm Monroe Sr.

Murder in the Hood

Tit for tat, you shoot at me, and I will shoot back.

You stepped on my foot the other night in the club; now, my brother,
you got to shed some blood.

The police showed up, nobody seen a thing.

Snitches get stitches, it's the code of the hood.

Somebody saw the shooter running in the woods.

My little sister's boyfriend was the one who was shot.

Now I gotta stay up all night and listen to her cry.

The undertaker gets rich while the young die.

Murder in the first degree is what the judge will say.

They say when you die, your soul will go free.

Balloons fly to heaven.

They put your picture on a t-shirt while another Black mother sits and cries.

Soon, they will forget your name.

Same time next week, another young Black will die.

You will have time to think about what you have done.

Was it worth it?

You just killed another Black mother's son.

You will not be going home tonight, all because you got into a fight.

Think you will never see your wife again.

Now she is sleeping in another man's arms.

Your daughter will walk down the aisle all by herself.

She will be thinking, "Why did my daddy leave?"

You will never see your son play another game.

It was your fault you did not leave a gun at home.

Who will be there to teach him how to be a man?

Will your future grandchildren understand why their grandfather went
into a rage and killed another man?

As you lay down on your bunk tonight, you better cry.

If you live a thousand years, you will be here until you die.

Run Uncle Buck, Run!

The word went out all over the land, the angels of God are looking far
a man named Buck Brown.

He escaped from Hell the other day.

Now Buck Brown is on the run, but Buck Brown is a part of my tree.

Wanted for sins he committed against the word of God.

They say Uncle Buck doesn't have a heart at all.

He lies.

He steals.

He cheats on his wife all the time.

He gets drunk, too.

Run, Uncle Buck, run.

One way or another, you'll be at Judgment Day!

No place to run.

No place to hide.

No matter what you do, the angels of God are looking for you.

No matter what, you will be in that line too.

All your relatives will be in line too.

Uncle Moonshine.

Cousin Gin.

Aunt Crack.

Uncle Blunt.

Your little brother Ice.

All will be standing in the line right behind you.

Run, Uncle Buck, run.

Somebody said you had bought yourself a gun; you got drunk and
walked all night.

Oh where, oh where have you gone Uncle Buck?

They say he went back to Hell and turned himself in.

They made him a trustee and gave him one wing, so now Uncle Buck can fly.

He won't escape again.

Fly, Uncle Buck. Fly with that one wing.

You won't fly too high.

Too Old to Live, Too Young to Die

When the years started to catch up with me, I could not do all the things
I used to do.

I could not walk as fast as I used to.

About this time, my eyes had started to go bad.

Sometimes I could not hear a lot of the words people would say.

The old mind had started to slip away.

They took away my driving license.

So one day my children came to me and said, "We are going to take all
your rights away. We are going to put you in a nursing home. That's
where old people belong, anyway!"

Too old to live, too young to die, just don't sit and wait to die.

Make death wait on you to say when you will bye-bye.

So whatever I got left, it may not be 100 percent, but at least it's 75
percent. So I am going to use it until there's nothing left.

Don't let nobody pour water on your fire.

Deep down in my heart, I want to be in love again.

I need somebody in my life to make me feel like a man.

To make me laugh out loud again.

I am fighting to live anyway I want to.

I am not going to let anybody tell me what to do.

They want to take whatever you got and put you away.

Sitting in a wheelchair and watching you fade away.

They will come to visit you on Thanksgiving Day.

They will tell your grandchildren you were just in the way.

You are so special! You were made by the hands of a living God.

Live! Live! Live! Live and don't let your children tell you what you
can or cannot do.

You are not too old to live!

Curtis Malcolm Monroe Sr.

Who cut out the lights?

Who cut the light out inside our schools, while our children lay down and bleed, their

Parents stand outside and scream.

Now what do you do next time they will shoot at you.

How do you stand inside and wash your hands while you hear bullets whizzing by?

Who cut the lights inside our malls, people spending their money, then have to run for their lives.

Who cut the lights out while the Devil walks the hallway?

Lord, have mercy; Jesus, don't all of them fall.

Who cut the lights out in Washington, DC, while we fight and brawl; the Statue of Liberty in the New York Harbor falls on her knees and cries out, "Let Freedom Ring!"

I know she wanted to die.

While powerful people wait for all to die.

They tell us to hate your fellow man.

We will let you vote if your color is right.

We won't let women make up their own minds; we're gonna fix it so you will have to hide in the night.

Who cut out the lights at the Supreme Court?

They sit back in their long black robes, and they let big businesses stick deadly chemicals up your nose.

They want to take away all of our rights.

Tell me, somebody, how do these people even sleep at night?

The 1950s have long passed us by.

They want to bring them back, why?

When the lights go out, can anyone see?

We all might as well be standing around like a dead tree. Who cut out the lights?

We took the truth and it's in jail.
We threw it right down to hell.
We tore up the Constitution and made a big old fire, took out a gun and
shot red, white, and blue.
Who cut out the lights down in the hood?
Black Lives Matter, but not to a lot of us.
We shoot a lot of our own with anger and hate, by our unforgiving
ways, and always just standing by.
How many of our young men have to die?
Who cut out the lights on our streets, when people of color have a target
on their backs?
Forty-nine bullets will take anyone's life.
Black mothers, I hear cries at night while sitting there thinking, *why
did they take my baby's life?*
Fly balloons fly, that's someone's life.
One more time, who cut out the lights in our hearts,
when we call each other names?
Cut the lights back on and let the eagles fly.
That will do, Curtis, that will do.

Nancy P. the Lioness

When she walked the halls of Congress, you would not hear her footsteps, but the thunder would rattle the floor. She had lightning tied around her neck, but it looked like a scarf, and when she spoke, all the windows shattered to the floor.

When she looked in your eyes, she would read your mind like a book. If you made her mad, you would hear a very loud roar, and everyone would clear the floor, and with nerves of steel she would never bend or break.

When she had to confront a man, she would treat them like a child. She made them think she would pull down and spank them like a child. She was the Speaker of the House; she was a lioness always in charge of her pride. Roar, Nancy! Roar! Everyone would get in line.

When all the men got under the table, she got up and stood right on top of it. She will point her finger right in your face. She never backs down.

When Obama came to the White House, he sent the lioness out, and when all the dust had settled once again, she stood above all the men, and they heard her roar once again. A lot of people did not like her, but Nancy did not give a damn. Superwoman in her cute little business dress; she could not fly, but she could if she wanted to.

Roar, Nancy, roar, make it very loud and clear. All the women of the world will be standing by your side. They say they want to kill her, hang her from a tree. Why in the world would anybody want to kill Nancy P.? She was only about five feet four or five inches tall, and maybe weighed, I would say, one hundred pounds. However, her shadow looms over thousands of miles.

Ping said to her, "Don't you come to Taiwan." The president said to her, "Nancy, please don't go. Ping, if you come, there will be war." But what did the lioness do? Nancy got on her plane and went anyway. I don't think she is mean, but don't tell Nancy P. what to do.

To all my fellow Americans, thank her for what she does. She is working hard for me and you. The Speaker of the House, the lioness. Everybody get back! Nancy P. is coming through. Hear Nancy P. roar. It is heard throughout the land but every time she roars, she does it with a smile. I could call her a woman, but I will leave that to you. She doesn't carry a rope, but she has a mean little finger.

Hear Nancy P. Roar! Hear her loud and clear! She roars for America and her pride too. Get in and just shut up and do what I tell you to do.

Roar, Nancy P.

Come and Walk with Me Down the J. D. Highway, M.W.A.

I want you to go with me, so please take my hand, close your eyes tight. I do not want you to see a single thing, and I will be your eyes. I only want you to pay attention to every word that I say.

Come on, my children, time to get under way; it's been a long and sad journey down the J. D. Highway, M.W.A.

Now take your earplugs out, I am going to tell you just what I see and hear.

I see big guns sitting on top of a hill.

I see men putting a big ball in and another man with a stick pushing something else in.

I see a man pulling on a string.

I see a lot of people fall.

I see bodies flying everywhere.

I see arms, legs, feet, and hands landing next to me. A man's head fell right on my shoe.

I see men running with stretchers to take the bodies away.

To the left I see a lot of small white tents.

In the back, dead bodies stacked as high as a tree.

I can hear them calling out to God. "Please save me, I want to go home to my son."

I hear crying out for their mothers, fathers, and little sisters too.

Walking down the J. D. Highway, M.W.A., put your earplugs back in and listen to the air.

Can you hear them?

Can you hear their pain and groans calling through the air?

Listen, I hear singing slaves standing by the road, "Swing low, sweet chariot, coming for to carry us home." While hundreds of dead are hanging from trees.

Thousands of little Black boys and girls standing around, trying to lift up their feet so they won't die.

The ground under their feet was soaking wet from their tears.

It was running down the street.

I don't want you to see their faces, but I want you to hear their pain.

The stars in the heavens had all started to cry; they were all tears of blood.

They cried so much it was a river of blood.

I ask myself if their deaths were right or wrong.

Come on walk a little bit further with me down the J. D. Highway, M.W.A., and see a big white door all trimmed in gold.

62,000 souls standing in line, all ready to go.

They all gave a last salute, and they were gone.

Take your earplugs out and open your eyes.

That will do, Curt, that will do.

Life is forever

There is not a worse feeling than when you know you are alone. When you are alone, when your heart cries out, *where has your family all gone?* You wake up in the middle of the night and there is no one left to answer your phone call. Your brother lay somewhere in a deep, cold hole. He cannot speak to you ever again. He will never be able to talk to you again. Never laugh with you again, while you sit and tell yourself one of his old lies. Remember this and remember that. Nothing else to remember. It's all in your mind. They have all left this world. All of their souls have flown away from this earth, and the other family that you thought you knew doesn't want anything to do with you. You call out to God and you ask him, *why?*

Now I cry all by myself in the middle of the night. I cry as loud as I can. Why? Because there is no one left to hear you walk the floor, and you cry out to God, "Why did you have to let my mother die?" All of my sisters and brothers have all gone away up there and are now facing the golden gates. Stop what you are doing and look up at the stars. Now pinch yourself and scream out loud and thank God you are still alive. It hurts so bad to know they won't be coming back. What am I going to do now? Walk around with your head hanging down; what would they want you to do? Whine, whine, whine. They would want you to spend the rest of your life thinking about them. I am hurting now, but God will not make me hurt forever. I will laugh again. I will smile again. I will love again. I will cry tears of joy. The sun will rise again as well as the moon, to give Mother Earth light on every dark night. God says we will live forever, that's why he gives us time to rest. I carry the memory of my family in my heart and my heart alone. I feel so much better since I wrote all of this down.

P. S. To all of my family that has passed away this year, you will always live in my heart forever.

Ernest T. Bass. All I Want Is a Girlfriend

The light shone down from the hills that night. A lot of bright lights were warning the town of Mayberry, that's right, Mayberry RFD. Tell the sheriff and deputy that the terror of the hills is on the way down. You could hear the crackling of trees falling to the ground. Thunder and lightning filled the air. Someone was saying out loud, "Yes, it's me. It's me. I am Ernest T. Bass. Take all of your women and all of your kids, lock all of your pets in the barn too. The hillbilly love machine is on the way."

So Andy called all the men in tow, and they all had to form some sort of defense to protect the town from Ernest T. Bass. Goober, Floyd, Otis, and Gomer all showed up. Everybody had a job to do. Some would stand on top of the courthouse with lookout glasses to see where Ernest T. could possibly be. Some roam the street with flashlights, just to be on the safe side.

Then they heard some glass break, and they knew Ernest T. had gotten into town. Then glass started to shatter everywhere, and Mrs. Crump came running out of her house, screaming and shouting that someone just threw a brick and broke her window out. They ran low to the ground to the squad car. She said that Ernest T. had tried to kiss her on the mouth. When Barney heard this, he went wild and started throwing karate chops and said that if he found Ernest T., he would nip him in the bud.

Then Floyd saw Ernest T. sitting on top of the sheriff's house. He had a jar of Aunt B.'s Pickles. They tasted so bad that they locked his jaw, and he fell from the top of the house. When he hit the ground, Barney put his one and only bullet in his gun. Out of nowhere, Otis came up and sat on top of him. So Andy told him to sit down and he had a talk with Ernest T. "What is wrong with you? Why do you keep coming to our town and busting our windows out?"

"Well, Sheriff, it's like this; all I want is a girlfriend. I went over to the Darlins' house and told Mr. Darlin that I came to see his daughter, Charlene. He said no straight to my face. So I ran out into the woods and sat in a tree and cried all night. When I went back the next day, that was a big mistake, because they beat me up and threw me in the hen house. I stayed there for three nights. Mr. Darlin came out of his house the next day and told me that if I came back again, he was going to sick his three mean dogs on me. That's when I decided I had better come to town. I wanted to get myself a uniform, so I can get a girlfriend."

So Andy sat there and thought for a while. "I'm going to see if I can get Alice Mae to go out with you. She is a short and stout girl. She's not ugly, but some people say she is wild. She is quick and really fast, but I'm telling you, Ernest T., you will have to run her down. If you can catch her, she will be your girlfriend for life. She lives down by Thelma's house. I will send Barney down there and see if he can flush her out. She has never had a boyfriend."

When Barney called out her name, she shot out of the house, running like a baby deer. So Barney called the sheriff and said to let Ernest T. out. So, Otis Campbell stood at the jailhouse door, waiting for Andy to say let her go. She ran by the jail like a bolt of lightning. Ernest T. was on her trail.

"My name is Ernest T. Bass, and I'm going to run you down." When there's a full moon in the hills, people say they saw them running through the trees. "My name is Ernest T. Bass, and I got myself a girlfriend."

*T*hompson station, the last plantation, threw the eyes of a child. A place that would drain the life out of your very soul. Malice and hate were the order of the day. Aches and pains were a way of life poor Black people standing in the sun, no place to run, no place to hide. Five years old with a sack on your back. Cold and wet, no shoes on your feet, no food to eat, not even a warm bed to sleep. And as a child, you began to cry. All you want to know is why. Your fingers are swollen and racked with pain, because no matter what you need to get the job done. Wagons filled with cotton roll by every day; little Black children sit on top, smiling all the way. Surprise, surprise, your daddy won't get paid today. Everything we worked hard for was taken away. You worked from sun to sun.

Walking behind a mule isn't no fun. Big pretty homes, big pretty cars, they all had everything they needed. While Black people were still on their knees. When people don't see you as a human being, these people can be so very mean. They took their welfare check. They took our hope, they took our pride, they took our dreams, they took our everything, and then they took the land. We had to give up everything to be poor. The richer get richer and the poorer get poorer. If for some reason we got out of line, the sheriff would come out and beat us own. Seven dollars a week, seven dollars a week, seven dollars a week, seven dollars a week, all she made was seven dollars a week. House filled with children, seven dollars a week. No food for the children to eat, no new shoes for their feet; poor things are freezing to death while they sleep. Every night train would go rolling by; your pride gets up and walks out the door. Old books and old clothing; you can't eat, trying to live off live off seven dollars a week. When Jesus comes back, he will be coming to Alabama first. Somebody got to pay for all their hate. Thompson station the last plantation, gone but not forgotten.

Curtis Malcolm Monroe Sr.

I Went out to Kill Union Springs

The night before, I went out to settle a beef about something dumb that happened on the street. Not a lot of money was at stake, but the burden carries a lot of weight. My wife burst into the room, and I tried to hide the blunt in my hand, but it was too late. My little girl asked me, "What was that smell, Daddy?" I did not know what to say. My wife looked at me and shook her head. I had taken my AK out and greased it up. I did not want it to misfire.

I thought about my target, and I knew where he lived, the man I was going to kill. If I have shot in his house, I will. I hit that blunt one more time. Went out and put that AK in the car. I sat there and wondered if they would shoot back. Will it be my funeral, or will it be his? About this time, my little boy jumped in my lap. What will happen to him if I do not come back home? Will he be raised by another man? Will he tell him how his father died with a gun in his hand? No matter what happens, I am on my way to Union Springs, and somebody is going to die. My hands got sweaty, and I started to wipe my forehead. My nerves were all over the place. I hit that blunt one time. So I pulled my car to the side, got out, opened the trunk, and pulled that AK out. I thought to myself, *I did not tell my wife goodbye.* This thing is starting to bother me. This man has a family just like me. I wonder how many kids he has. I wonder if he has a wife. They say that Black Lives Matter, but not to me. Here I am, ready to kill another Black man over a sack of weed. I let my pride get the better of me. Suddenly we roll into town, and the sign says, "City Limit of Union Springs." Now the hunt begins. I am going to hunt the boys down. I know what kind of car he has. I looked to the left, and I spotted his car. I parked outside the convenience store, and I grabbed my AK and blasted away. Bullets went flying everywhere. People were hollering and screaming. I did not blame who I hit. I got my revenge and left. I went to Union Springs because I was out to kill. I knew one day they would come for me. Then for a long time I wouldn't be free. By that time my child would have forgotten about me. I think about the people I shot. I can't take it back. What is done is done. They should put me against the wall and shoot me down. I pray to God I hadn't ever shot that gun. Somewhere in that small town, people are putting their loved ones in the ground. Holding each other's hands, asking themselves *why?*

Children without a father.

Wife without a husband.

Grandfather without granddaughter.

Uncles without nephews.

Cousins without cousins.

Sisters without sisters.

Brothers without brothers.

When I got in that car, I did not give a damn who lived or died. Now I am sitting here waiting for a tapping to come to my door, a loud call out of "Put your hands up! We are going to read you your rights and take you away." I wish I had not gotten in that car that day, but that's the price I will have to pay, because I went out to kill.

The Big Elephant

It was time for the Iron Bowl; Auburn and Alabama would fight for the crown again. Who would be the big dog in the state once again? Both of the teams had run out on the field, and both were ready to fight it out. The fans were yelling at the top of their lungs. Then it was time for the teams to come out. The Tiger came out, wagging his tail, talking, growling, and making noise with his claws when they would hit the ground, while sparks were shooting out from everywhere he struck the floor. About this time the eagle flew in, red and white; his wings were stretched as far as they could go. He landed right on the tiger's back! It was time for the eagle to talk trash, "Where is that fat elephant at? I guess he is too ashamed to show his face! Hey, fat boy! We're going to kick your fat tail again! Since elephants never forget, do you remember that run down the sideline? Did you bring your fat wife and your ugly kids? I am surprised they are not holding your tail again. Why do elephants like to smell each other's butts? Big old nose, an ugly snout, with ears so big they block out the sun, big feet with ugly toenails, you should have gone down to the creek and washed your ass. You smell so bad. I can smell you five miles in the air. Where are you at, fat boy? Come out on the field. Auburn is gonna kick Alabama's ass again!"

The whole stadium began to shake. The sound could be heard for a hundred miles. As the fans sat in their seats, they began to cheer and clap their hands. The walls had begun to crack and break, and dust was flying everywhere. The tiger and the eagle looked at each other straight in the face! Don't look dumb now, the elephant was on his way. He stopped and stomped his feet. People were losing their false teeth. He took his big snout out and threw it up in the air. The sound he made could be heard all over the United States. "I heard what you said about me, and I am here today to straighten the record out." He looked the tiger and the eagle right in their eyes. They were so afraid they started to cry. They knew they were in for the fight of their lives. "I was asleep, but you two woke me up." The tiger went in first, right for the elephant's feet. The elephant used his snout and caught him by the tail, slammed him to the ground about ten to twelve times. The tiger screamed out in terrible pain. His tail was bent in three or four places. He could not wag his tail again. Bang! Bang! He did it again, tight and nowhere to run. All of his stripes filled the air. You could hear bones begin to crack as he tried to get up. Poor little tiger looked like a little rag doll. Then the eagle came in from the air. He misjudged, it was bad, and stuck his head in the elephant's behind. What a terrible place to be, because the elephant had to use the restroom.

When the eagle hit the ground, he was not red and white anymore; he was brown. Then the eagle started to cry and asked himself, "What the hell am I doing here? Tiger, you are on your own. Don't look for me, I'll be over at the toilet paper tree." The big elephant won the fight that day. Auburn got a good beating on the field that day.

"Come back again next year! I'll be waiting to do it all over again!"

Curtis Malcolm Monroe Sr.

They Call It Country Music

When we were little boys growing up, all we had was a little black-and-white TV with a bent piece of wire for an antenna. Mama would make us two large burgers and a large plate of fries. That's when we knew she was going out, because she would turn on the TV. We could only get one channel, and I believe it was channel 12. We sat there and watched the *Porter Wagoner Show;* we didn't know who these people were, and they sure did wear fancy clothes. Their outfits sure did sparkle and glitter as they moved around, and they all wore big cowboy hats and fancy cowboy boots. Almost all of them had pretty guitars to play also. After listening for a while, they made us start to pat our feet to the rhythm. This lady with a head full of blond hair, we had never seen a woman with hair like that before, and she had a beautiful dress on. Then this lady with a funny little hat on top of her head with the price tag on it still came on; sometimes with an old guy they called Grandpa. Then Conway Twitty came out and sang about a girl wearing tight-fitting jeans. We didn't understand what he was talking about, but as we got older, we figured it out. This man who was tall with black hair started singing about standing in a ring of fire. We thought about it for a while. Why would anyone want to stand in a ring of fire? Then this man with long braided hair said he saw two angels flying too low to the ground. So we went outside, and we looked for them. A coal miner's daughter, she had a beautiful voice. We saw a man called the Possum who wanted to know who would fill his shoes. Then Lester and Earl told a story about when a hillbilly found oil in their field. He had a daughter who could throw a rock a hundred of miles. They had this lady who made us cry. She had a picture of another woman with her man. Some of them said they wanted to cry. Then we saw a snaggle-toothed mule, people standing in a cornfield, and then we looked again, and we saw Goober. They call it country music. We did not know that, but come next Saturday night, we will be watching again.

I remember the say she was born, the nurse put her in my arms.

I looked down in at a tiny little face as tears
rolled down my face.

Ten little fingers and ten little toes, little round
nose.

Tiny, perfect, beautiful, red little ears, didn't
have much hair, but it was enough.

When she cried I could hear the Angels in
heaven sing.

Small in stature just a handful.

Her eyes were bright as the sun and her smile
could melt the snow.

I got in trouble and had to go away.
When I got back, my baby was gone.
Can anybody tell me where my baby has gone?
Somebody told me she got in with the wrong
crowd and was led astray.

I don't know.

She looks like she all grown now.

People, my baby girl is gone.

They say they saw her over here, saw her over there.

It's my fault things went wrong for her.

I call myself a man.

I should have been there for her.

Is somebody beating her up, taking advantage
of her love and using her in every bad way?

Is she now somebody's sex slave? How many
times has she called my name?

My father should have been there to protect
me from all these dangerous things.

Mother told me my Daddy is a real man.

Has anyone seen my little girl?

I got a call out of the blue from a longtime
friend of mine one day.

Told me your daughter is up here walking the
streets in a place called Union Springs.

So I got in the car and drove as fast as I could.

I had to get there. I got there, I had left so fast,
her Mother had not even given her a name.

So, I looked around to see if I could recognize
her face.

I saw a young girl walking to a car as she
reached for the door, I called out her mother's name.

She stopped right in her tracks.

I could she was thinking who the hell are you?

She had her mother's face. I had to stop and cry.

Standing there I dropped my head in pain.

I had my baby girl.

The way she was dressed, she didn't say a thing.

She was getting ready to leave with a man. So
I reach out and touched her by the hand.

I pulled her close to me and whispered in her
ear, "Daddy's home. You do not have to do this
no more."

She said to me, "Daddy, where have you been
for so long? I cried myself to sleep every night
calling out your name. I'm sorry Daddy you had
to see this. After Mother passed away, I didn't
know what else to do."

Then she asked me, "Daddy can I go home with
you please, Daddy?"

Written by
Curtis Monroe,
Alabama

9 798890 272720